BETTER THAN BLENDED

WORKBOOK

Revised Edition

BETTER THAN BLENDED WORKBOOK
Revised Edition
A Study to Help Blended Families Grow
Closer to Each Other and Become More
Intentional in Their Interactions

BY WILLIE AND RACHEL G. SCOTT

A Better than Blended Family Ministries book published by Team Kingdom Impact Publishing, LLC.

PO Box 18699 Cleveland Heights, OH 44118

The material in appendix 1 is from HelpGuide.org and is used by permission.

Printed in the United States of America 24 23 22 21 20 19 18 17 16 1 2 3 4 5 6

ISBN-13 (trade paper): 978-0-9973626-5-7

Library of Congress Control Number: 2017911606

Editing by Rebecca English of Gladbooks Editorial Services

Cover design by Jesus Cordero

Back cover photo by Autumn Scott

Antonio, Willie III, Autumn, Dominique, Darius, Gabrielle, and Aaron, we love all of you and we are eternally thankful that we get to call you our children!

CONTENTS

FOREWORD

BY MARK TIMM

Among the many undeniable truths of life, consider these three:

Truth #1: In a perfect world, there wouldn't need to be a book about blended families.

Truth #2: We don't live in a perfect world, so a book designed to help families navigate the blending process is sorely needed!

I'm the father of a family of six kids. When my wife Ann and I were married, we each brought three children to our new family, so I've been in the blended business for several years now. Which leads me to…

Truth #3: Blending families isn't easy!

Fortunately, Willie and Rachel G. Scott, founders of Better than Blended, have stepped up with this fantastic resource you're holding in your hands right now.

As soon as I read the first chapter, I immediately began thinking how much this workbook would have helped my family a few years ago when we first came together.

Our experience was—to put it mildly—a bit bumpy. We were all fully committed to coming together, but it was the little things that caught us by surprise and sometimes grew into bigger things when we let them go unaddressed.

For example, before Ann came into the picture, my kids and I were not nutrition-savvy at meal times. Not at all. I knew that we needed to eat some good meals, but as far as I was concerned, a box of macaroni and cheese or a can of ravioli counted as home-cooked goodness!

On the other hand, Ann is the Organic-Whole-Food-Nutrition-Queen. Frankly, I'm not sure she's ever even seen canned ravioli, much less consumed one. So when she took over the kitchen, let's just say the three kiddos I brought to the family didn't wholeheartedly embrace the leafy greens and ancient grains on the table.

Of course, Ann and I each had to re-learn how to communicate effectively as a couple without bringing in baggage and assumptions from the broken down communications of our previous marriages.

No doubt about it: successfully blending families is not easy. But the Scotts bring good news. It can be done. And it can be done well.

The ideas and principles the Scotts share in this Better than Blended Workbook can be valuable at any time in the process, not only at the beginning. Ann and I are reaping additional benefits from it even now, years after we started this blended family journey.

Useful, practical, and user-friendly, this workbook will empower your family to be, do, and have more of all life has to offer. First, Willie and Rachel share their insights on wide-ranging topics relevant to blended families: managing conflict, recognizing past hurts, keeping your spousal relationship first, navigating the stepparent role, discipline, intentional family time, and much more.

The second section of each chapter introduces thought-provoking discussion questions designed for couples or small groups. You'll get the opportunity here to do a deeper dive into your own situation to understand your paradigms and behaviors.

Finally, each chapter concludes with a practical application section, chock-full of suggestions for specific actions for real, positive changes in the blended family dynamic.

This workbook is a transformational tool and the Scotts have done a tremendous service to families by creating it. The fact that you've picked it up means you're invested in making your family life all that it can be. Congratulations!

I encourage you to spend the time, really dig into the material, and then commit to the suggested action steps to help your family win consistently.

Your better-than-blended family is 100% percent worth it!

Mark Timm
Executive Vice President, Ziglar Inc.
CEO, Ziglar Family
www.ziglarfamily.com

PREFACE
WELCOME TO BETTER THAN BLENDED

When two people meet and fall in love, they typically don't take the time to fully consider the extent to which their love will change their lives. During a beautiful marriage ceremony, they stand before witnesses and confess their undying love and vow their commitment to one another. All the decorations and ceremonial pomp, however, don't prepare them for the hard work that lies ahead.

This is especially true for couples whose marriage will create a blended family—a joining together of his children and her children into one new family. Blended families bring to the altar hopes and dreams of a family that will become one. But those hopes and dreams can be dashed by the reality that getting the whole family on board with the couple's love isn't as easy as saying "I do" and then "you do too."

This was our story. As children, we both experienced life in blended-family homes and were exposed to the challenges of being in a blended family at an early age. When we joined together in marriage (Willie had three children, and Rachel had two), we desired to be better than the blended families we had experienced growing up. We desired to become one family! This was an audacious goal—but not impossible. We now have a total of seven children ranging in age from toddler to adult. Our testimony as one family has led to the birth of

our organization, Better than Blended, and become a catalyst toward redemption for blended families who are struggling to find common ground.

Our story is full of wisdom that we have gained through both mistakes and victories, and we want to share that wisdom with you.

We also want to encourage and remind you that blending into a family that walks in unity, even when the path gets difficult, is possible.

It is a journey—one that will have some steep valleys of seeming defeat as well as high mountains of apparent victories. But it is worth it!

Strong blended families aren't the result of some magic pill or a single prayer. Strong blended families are the result of hard work and applied wisdom! We hope that you will find both of them in this study. This workbook presents a combination of applying truth to your lives, learning to be intentional in creating effective family practices, and using wisdom to move your family from simply being blended to being better than blended.

What does it mean to be better than blended? It means more than surviving—it means thriving! It means becoming a blended family that is actually one. It means becoming a family that is a pillar of strength and that develops an awesome testimony to the sustaining power of intentionality and truth.

As you and your spouse begin and complete the Better than Blended Workbook, we would love to see three main goals achieved:

1. Enhance your blended-family experience by drawing closer to each other as a family.

2. Strengthen your blended family by helping your children develop heartfelt relationships with each other for the future.

3. Be intentional about developing unity and oneness in every aspect of your blended family.

This study is a curriculum for couples seeking to raise blended families in a unified and productive manner, but it is more than that. It is a template for you and your spouse to create and chronicle your story together and to share your testimony with other couples in a way that will help you identify how you became better at blending. Be ready to share this resource with another couple when you've completed it!

The workbook contains six sessions designed to be completed over a six-week period (each spouse should have his or her own workbook). It is intended to be done in a group setting with a leader (you will find a leader's guide at the back of this workbook), but it could just as easily be done with a few couples gathering together or even with one couple at home. Each session is intended to last approximately an hour and a half and is broken into three sections:

1. Discovery (30 to 45 minutes): Consider what's hindering your family from blending better.

2. Discussion (30 to 45 minutes): Talk with your spouse and other couples about how what you've discovered applies to your situation.

3. Application (at home): Ask yourself, what will we do differently now in our family?

Wherever you are as a blended family, if you as a couple desire unity and oneness, then engaging in this training with open hearts and minds will take your family to the next level. We hope that a deepened sense of purpose for your family will take root in your hearts and that the fruit of your love for each other, your children, and truth will yield a family that is better than blended.

1

WRITING OUR OWN BLENDED FAMILY STORIES

The last page turned is a perfect excuse to write a whole new book.

Toni Sorensen

Whether you are on the road to becoming a blended family, have just become a blended family, or have been part of a blended family for many years, you have probably at one time or other asked, "How does this work?" Chances are, you hope for or have worked for a smooth transition and a happy family life for you, your spouse, and your children, but you also know that things are not always that easy. Adjusting to married life can be a big challenge in itself, but when we add children to the mix, things can become a lot more complicated.

So many things have been taught and suggested about how to become a blended family. In all likelihood, we've all heard well-meaning comments from people like, "It's so great that you'll be able to fill a parental void in your stepchildren's lives!" or "Your kids must be so excited to have new siblings!" or "Your family will be just like the Brady Bunch." Many of the things we hear, however, are myths, opinions, or simply speculations.

Not only do other people's opinions affect our outlook, but our own expectations can also derail us when it comes to what we think our blended-family experience should be like. The way we were raised, especially if we ourselves grew up in a blended family, often forms much of our perspective as to how we think our family will function.

The fact is, none of people's various ideas nor our own past experiences can explain exactly what our blended-family experience should look like.

Becoming a blended family has its fair share of challenges, but it is possible to navigate this journey well and gracefully. The truth is, with wisdom and some intentional effort on our part, we can create a unified family, no matter what others say or do and no matter what our own experiences were.

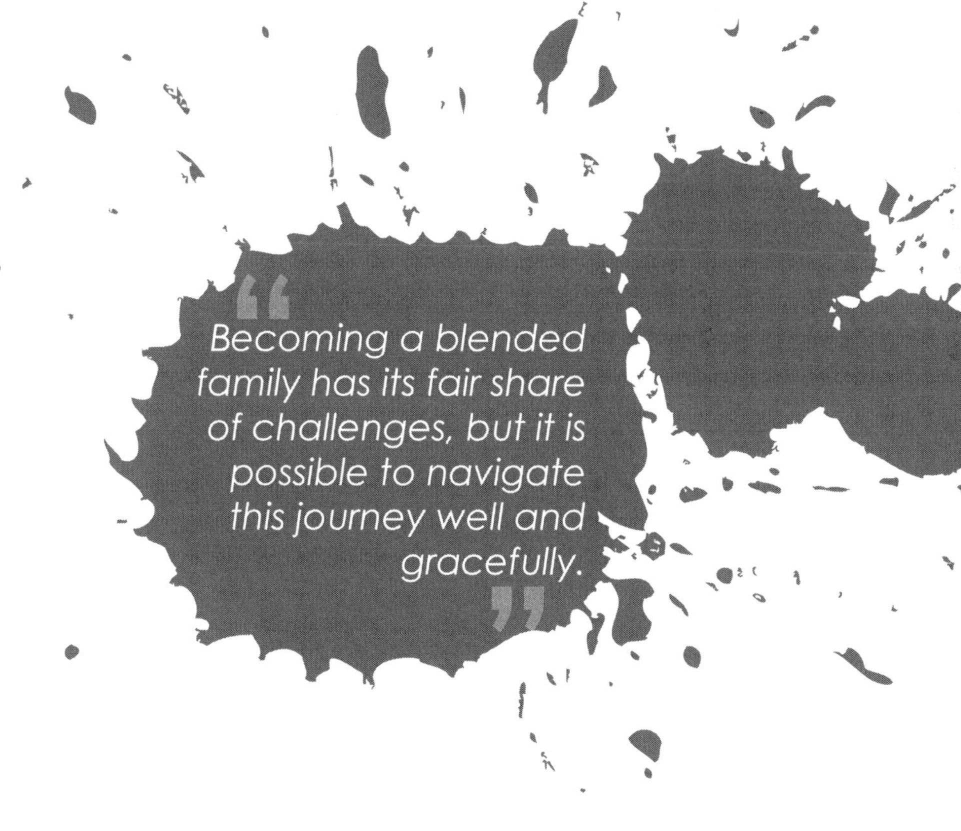

DISCOVERY
CONSIDER WHAT IT MEANS TO BLEND BETTER

CREATING OUR OWN STORIES—A BETTER WAY

All of us have developed ideologies about being a blended family, whether they are based on others' ideas or on our own past experiences. It is important for us to identify any false expectations we hold and remove them from our minds so that we can start over with a clean slate and write a new story for our own blended families.

OTHER PEOPLE'S OPINIONS SHAPE OUR IDEOLOGIES

Stories and advice from others do not make up our stories. When it comes to ideologies about blended families, we really can't debunk them, because the ideas may be true for some people. What we can do, however, is determine that no matter where we may be in blending our families, we want to create our own stories. It is okay to glean wisdom from other people's stories, because we may gain some needed light from them in certain areas of our family, but taking their stories and owning them for ourselves is a mistake we can easily make. Stories and advice from other people are not our own stories.

One of the primary features of being a blended family is that many outside influences can affect the process of a family becoming one. Ex-husbands or ex-wives, former in-laws, or any other affiliation from previous relationships can potentially affect the blending process. Yet the blessing in being a blended family is a chance to start fresh and new—to create new memories, traditions, and ways of life. New norms are often the result of blending a family, and in many cases it's a chance to start our stories over.

Today is the day to start your story! Your story will not be based on your past or on what others have told you but on what you desire your blended family to become.

OUR OWN EXPERIENCES SHAPE OUR EXPECTATIONS

We all have stories that, if revealed, would explain a lot about who we are now. For those of us who have experienced being in a blended family, we can't help but shape our expectations around what we know. For those who haven't been in a blended family, your expectations may be shaped around what you have heard or assume things will be like. Either experience is a good place to start, but remember this: our experiences shape our expectations.

One of the first steps toward writing our own family's story is to identify what we expect our blended family to look, feel, and act like. We need to identify what expectations we have—which may or may not be realistic—and the basis for them.

In doing that, we need to remember that how we grew up affects the way we view blending. Sometimes we don't notice how our upbringing influences our current family interactions or decisions, but it's important for us to recognize that it's a major factor.

As we look back at our childhood and identify the reasons behind our expectations, it will greatly help us in our blending process, because it will help us to identify which of our expectations are realistic and which may not be.

Sometimes we have created massive expectations in order to guard our hearts from the unknown, and this can be detrimental to the goal of family oneness. We need to be open to our own blended-family walk, however the journey may look.

THE RIGHT WAY TO BLEND

The truth is, there is no perfect way to blend, but there is a better way!

Though *we* may be totally caught off guard by the circumstances that led us to this blended lifestyle or to the circumstances surrounding us as blended families, we can rest assured that there is nothing new under the sun. Although divorce ultimately is not desirable, not everyone is willing to work through difficult things in a marriage. Sometimes a marriage can be so destructive to a person physically, mentally, emotionally, and spiritually that being released from the marriage is absolutely necessary. In other cases our youthful choices or extenuating circumstances led us to where we are now, or perhaps we arrived here with a widowed heart that still desires to love.

No matter what our story is, grace is available on our blending journeys. Through learning how to operate in truth and intentionally seeking wisdom, the path to blending will become clear.

CREATING FAMILY UNITY

The better way of blending leads to family unity—but it requires some intentionality on our part.

Have you ever been talking to someone and had to explain the "yours, mine, and ours" scenario? It looks a little like this: "Well, Joe was mine before I remarried, and Bill had two kids from his previous marriage, and then we had one together." We always seem to end with an awkward pause and a half smile. Especially if the kids are standing there. And all the person asked is if all these kids were ours.

How do we think our stepchildren feel when we go through this long explanation? Especially if one of their birth parents isn't in their lives? What if they want to look at us as parents?

This has happened to us (Willie and Rachel) on one too many occasions, but we decided early on that we would eliminate all blended-family jargon unless it was absolutely necessary. Most of the time people have no idea that ours is a blended family. It's not because all our kids call us Mom and Dad or because we all look alike; it's because if people ever ask if our kids are our children, our first and most common response is yes.

We don't go into a long explanation—we just leave it there.

If we want to blend in a better way, we need to remember this: being better than blended means taking every step possible to create unity where division would desire to creep in. We have to ask the right people for help, seek wisdom, and be intentional about becoming one as a family.

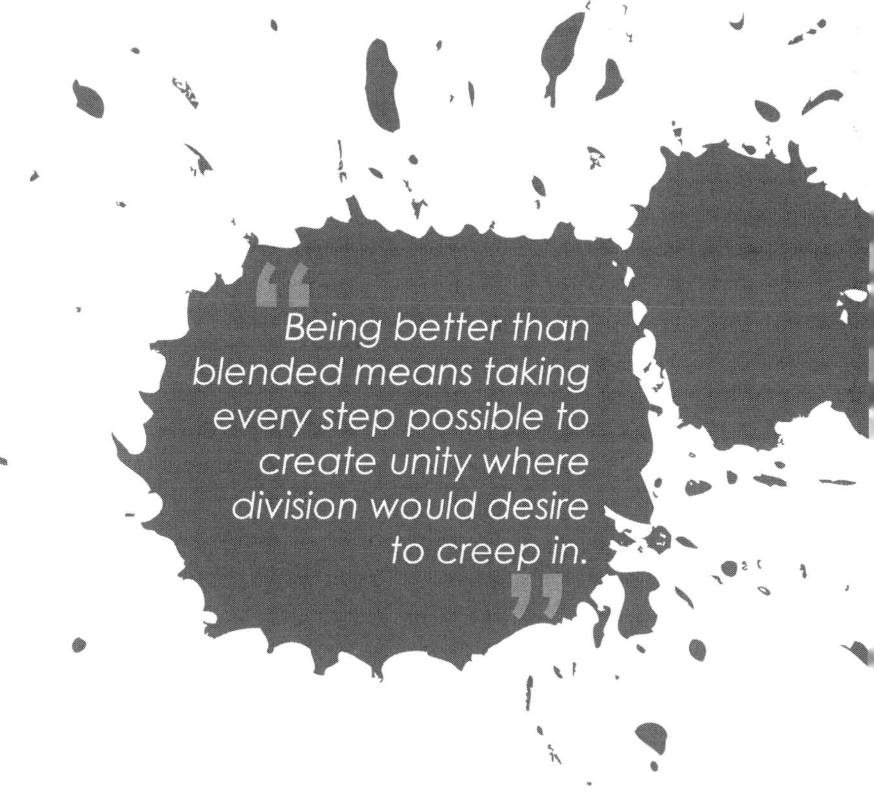

If our goal is to become a unified family, then the cliché of "yours, mine, and ours" must be adjusted.

"Yours" and "mine" should be removed so that "ours" stands alone. It is almost impossible for us to begin to develop a relationship with our stepchildren if we create a clear separation between our kids and our spouse's kids. We have to remember that although the children may be our spouse's, we now have the opportunity to help raise and transform their lives. Our spouse is no longer in this boat alone, and neither are we.

You see, children know when we are not fully invested in building a relationship with them. Learning to embrace them all as "ours" breaks down walls and shows our kids that regardless of when they decide to embrace our blended family, we are already committed to them. This is the better way! And our kids need to see this.

Yes, our hearts may get broken and our feelings may get hurt a few times. It may feel as if we're swimming upstream, and we're tired and would prefer to simply go with the flow. But we can take comfort in knowing that one day our children will be wiser and will look back at our relationship with them and truly know that we were always there for them—and that we not only spoke truth but also lived out our blended-family experience intentionally.

That's the message we want them to see.

DISCUSSION:
HOW DOES THIS APPLY TO OUR SITUATION?

It's time to talk about what we've learned! Pair up with one or two other couples to answer and then discuss the questions below. (If you are uncomfortable talking with others or if you are doing this study at home, you can do this section with just your spouse.) Take ten to fifteen minutes to write your answers individually to the questions below, and then take an additional twenty to thirty minutes to discuss your answers with your spouse and the others in your group.

1. What are some wrong ideologies that you believe or have believed in the past about being a blended family?

2. What does having a clean slate look like for you?

3. Based on your own past experience, what expectations might you have about becoming a blended family?

4. What do you love about your family dynamic? What are some challenges you face right now in becoming one family?

5. How have you learned to embrace "ours"? If you haven't, what is holding you back?

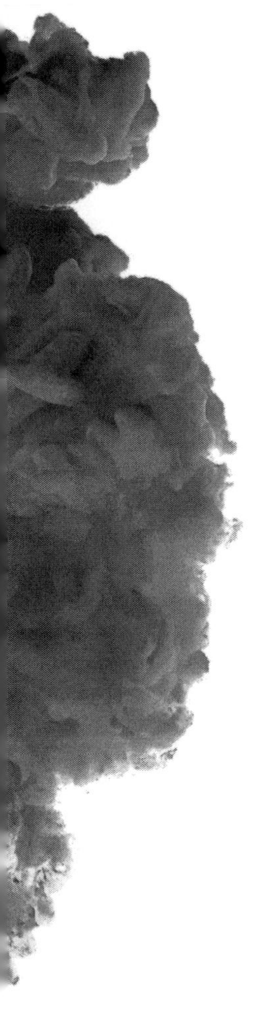

APPLICATION:

WHAT WILL WE DO DIFFERENTLY NOW?

Session 1 focused on discovering your own blended-family story. This week at home, before coming back for session 2 next week, set aside some time to complete the action activity below as a couple.

Each spouse should be allowed to explain his or her thoughts regarding the following questions and/or activities. Speak honestly. Listen to each other respectfully.

1. Honestly assess your family and then decide which of the following statements best describes your situation:

    Two separate families

    Fluctuating between blended and separate

    One blended family

2. Based on your answers, what is one goal that you as a couple have for your family? Record your goal in the space below.

As you wrap up your application time together as a couple, spend some time together discussing the goal for your family that you recorded above. We have provided a couple's affirmation below to meet you where you are as you finish session 1.

You can close with an affirmation of your own, or you can use this one:

We agree that we have been brought together for a purpose. We will seek our divine purpose in every aspect of our family. We will seek guidance and direction as we work to become one family. We will treat both our family's need for growth and its successes with the same enthusiasm. We will be a family that is intentional and purposeful in our interactions with each other, treating one another as we would want to be treated. Our family will embrace truths and each other daily. Our family will become one.

Commit to saying this affirmation together at least once more this week.

2

DEALING WITH CONFLICT

People generally fall into one of three groups: the few who make things happen, the many who watch things happen, and the overwhelming majority who have no notion of what happens. Every person is either a creator of fact or a creature of circumstance. He either puts color into his environment, or, like a chameleon, takes color from his environment.

Dr. Myles Munroe

Parenting within a blended family is much different than in a traditional family. In a blended family, besides dealing with the ordinary challenges of growing up, our children also have to contend with additional external influences. Added to the vast changes that already exist in trying to become a blended family, children of blended families experience many situations due to these outside influences that can affect their attitude within the family. This has the potential to generate a great deal of conflict in the home.

DISCOVERY

UNDERSTANDING HOW TO KEEP PEACE IN THE HOME

Some of the outside influences in our children's lives are their other parents, their relatives, and friends and acquaintances from earlier in their lives. Any of these relationships can have a major impact on our children's efforts to integrate into our blended family. Besides these outside influences, a child's age, gender, and stage of life also have a great deal to do with how he or she adjusts to life in our home and can contribute to the potential for family conflict.

AN ABSENT PARENT

Some children of blended families have two sets of parents who are an active part of their daily life. Both sets of parents participate in the upbringing of the child and carry similar expectations as to what they desire for the child to accomplish by adulthood. Unfortunately, this is not most commonly the case. Much more often children of blended families are raised primarily in the household of one birth parent and have little interaction with the other birth parent.

A parent who is not an active part of his or her child's day-to-day life and activities as a parent should be is what we call an absent parent. How do we deal with the absent parent? While there are a number of guidelines for interacting well with an absent parent, the bottom line is this: the key to raising children with an absent parent is always to seek what is in the best interest of the children.

This may not always look the same from one family to another.

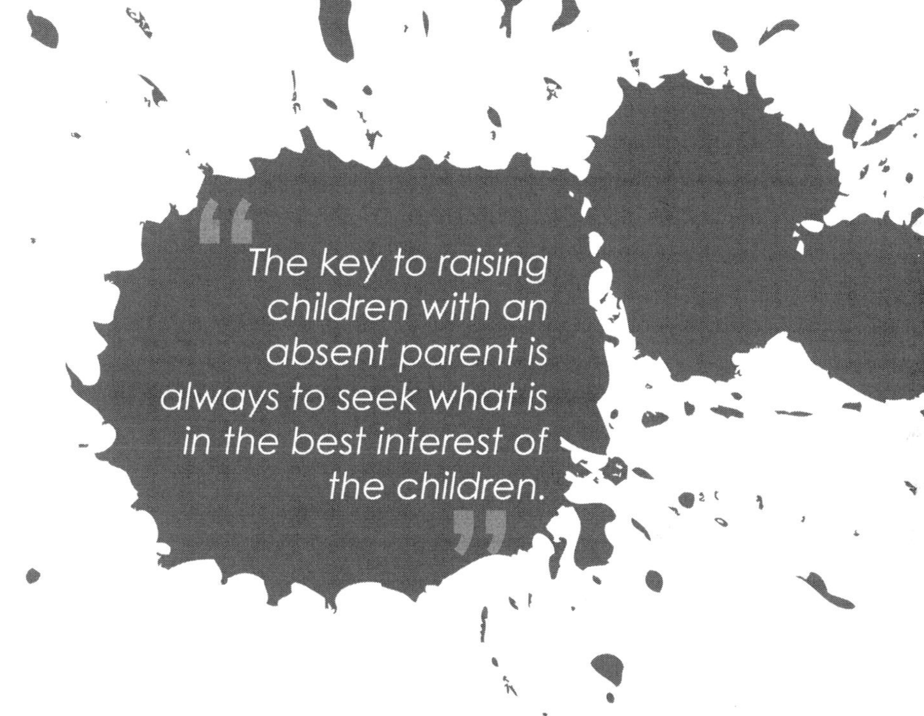

(For practical tips on maintaining a peaceful scenario with an absent parent, we have provided an amazing resource, *7 Ways to Deal with Conflict in Co-Parenting,* that blended families may use as a tool and reference guide in learning to deal with the absent parent and the conflicts that may arise within the parenting journey.[1])

OTHER OUTSIDE INFLUENCES

Perhaps your child doesn't have an absent parent, but maybe you deal with other outside influences, such as an active parent, grandparent, aunt, or uncle. All these people care about the well-being of your child, but they all have a different perspective on how the child should be raised. While these people are rightly part of our children's lives, it is important that we have a clear understanding of who may be influencing our children and how that influence may be impacting the dynamic of the home.

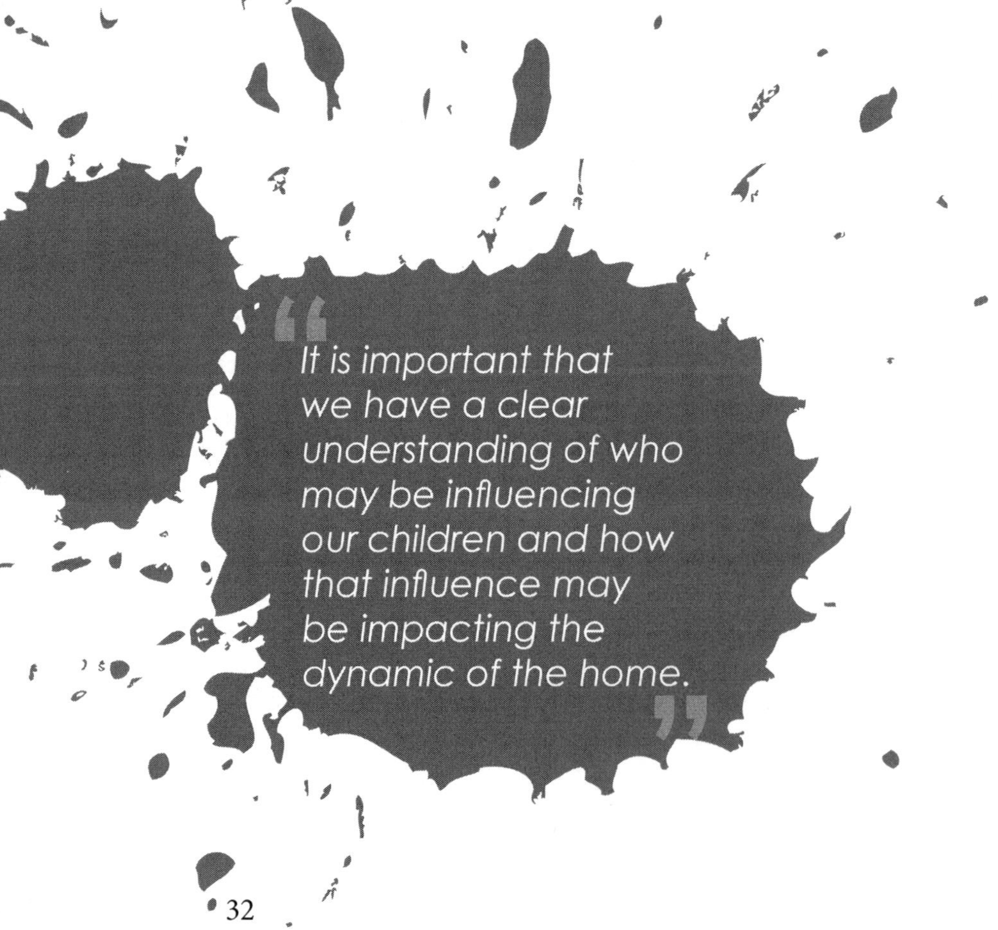

Once we establish who is influencing our children, we must become aware of what we want our children's experience in our home to look like and then set boundaries that will guard that experience.

For example, Lisa and Bill have a blended family with four children (two are Lisa's, and two are Bill's). Bill's previous wife passed away, and prior to his meeting Lisa, the children's maternal grandmother went over and above to compensate for the children's mom being gone. Bill was fine with that and allowed the children to go to her home whenever she asked. But when Bill remarried, the children embraced Lisa and enjoyed spending time with her. Bill and Lisa and the kids began doing things as a family, and Bill had to say no at times when the grandmother asked if the kids could come over.

Over time Bill and Lisa noticed a shift in the children's attitude whenever they returned from visiting their grandmother, especially when after visits the children would go back and forth between calling Lisa "Mom" and calling her "Mrs. Lisa." One day the grandmother asked to take the children out of town for a holiday, and Bill stated no, they would be spending the holiday together as a family. The grandmother became upset and began to let Bill know how she felt.

At that moment Bill's thoughts that the children's attitudes were being influenced by the grandmother were confirmed. Bill and Lisa made a decision to restructure the relationship with his former mother-in-law in an attempt to protect their family's blending process. They did not stop the children from going to the grandmother's home, but they minimized the occurrences and maximized their family time.

A home should be a safe haven for anyone who enters, especially the people who live within it. That includes us! Every relationship isn't a healthy one for our children or for our homes. We must recognize which relationships may need some restructuring to fit the new pace and tone of our home.

HOW AGE, GENDER, AND STAGE AFFECT CHILDREN

When we (Willie and Rachel) first began blending our families, we were met with many new challenges and frustrations. Each of our children seemed to adjust differently to the new family dynamic, some better than others.

Studies have shown that children respond to the new adult in their lives differently based on age and gender. Here are some thoughts to consider from HelpGuide. org:

Kids of different ages and genders will adjust differently to a blended family. The physical and emotional needs of a two-year-old girl are different than those of a thirteen-year-old boy, but don't mistake differences in development and age for differences in fundamental needs. Just because a teenager may take a long time accepting your love and affection doesn't mean that he doesn't want it. You will need to adjust your approach with different age levels and genders, but your goal of establishing a trusting relationship is the same.[2]

The stage of life that a child is in—meaning where a child is in perceiving his or her own identity—also greatly impacts how that child will adjust to being part of a blended family. Toddlers, who receive most of their identity from parents, caregivers, and older siblings, will adjust to being part of a blended family much differently than will teenagers, who receive most of their identity from their peers and other outside influences. (For more details on how age and stage of identity affect a child's adjustment to being part of a blended family, see appendixes 1 and 2.)

When adjusting to being part of a blended family, children will take in their new situation in light of what is going on in their personal lives.

Having an understanding of the ages, genders, and stages the children in your home are in will help you better understand their potential frustrations and minimize the possibility of conflict.

THE PEACE THERMOSTAT

One of the most important things we can do is decide with our spouse where we want the "peace thermostat" of our home to be set. Many things may try to disrupt the peace within our homes, but we should do all we can to live at peace with everyone. This means being intentional to define clear ways of creating peace, and when we do this, it will help us "reset the temperature" when it has been moved from its setting of peace.

Here are a few tips to help maintain peace in the home:

1. Have a time of family encouragement every Saturday or Sunday (or on a day when all or most kids are present in the home) to set the thermostat for the week.

2. Have a family meeting and review the expectations for the week (regarding homework, chores, technology, etc.). Discuss how you can

support each other and how everyone's roles are important to the family.

3. Have a word or phrase that everyone in your home uses when peace seems to be fading. Allow the family member who is best at keeping peace in the home to create the word. This will show your humility in admitting that you as a parent are not perfect and will allow the family member to be recognized for his or her great work in keeping peace in the home.

4. Engage in activities to help build unity in the home so that your children learn that unity and peace go hand in hand. (A good example of a fun activity is a game of volleyball, parents against kids.)

DISCUSSION:

HOW DOES THIS APPLY TO OUR SITUATION?

It's time to talk about what we've learned! Pair up with one or two other couples to answer and then discuss the questions below. (If you are uncomfortable talking with others or if you are doing this study at home, you can do this section with just your spouse.) Take ten to fifteen minutes to write your answers individually to the questions below, and then take an additional twenty to thirty minutes to discuss your answers with your spouse and the others in your group.

1. What are your interactions with ex-spouses, parents of your stepchildren, or in-laws like? Which relationships are healthy? Which relationships are in need of restructuring?

2. What are some of the ways you handle what other people say or think about your family?

3. What boundaries have you established to appropriately protect your home from outside influences? What boundaries might you need to set?

4. What ages, genders, and stages are the children in your home? How does recognizing this help you understand some of the ways your children are handling your family's blending process?

5. What temperature is your peace thermostat most commonly set on? What adjustments can you and your spouse make to reset the temperature when necessary?

APPLICATION:
WHAT WILL WE DO DIFFERENTLY NOW?

Session 2 focused on keeping peace in the home and resolving conflict in a blended family. This week, before coming back for session 3, set aside some time at home to complete the action activity below as a couple.

Each spouse should be allowed to explain his or her thoughts regarding the following questions and/ or activities. Speak honestly. Listen to each other respectfully.

1. What affects the peace thermostat in your home?

2. Take a moment to evaluate your family. Identify three things that have caused conflict most often in your family. (Besides outside influences and children's ages, genders, and stages, this could be things like finances, discipline of children, need for intimacy, communication, faith, work, etc.) Write them below.

3. What are three strategies or steps you will put into action to help ensure that the conflicts in your family are addressed properly? Record your answers below.

4. Revisit the family goal you made in session 1, and decide how to take an additional step to reach that goal. Before meeting for session 3, find an accountability couple, and share your family goal with them.

As you wrap up your application time together as a couple, spend some time together discussing the developing goal you have for your family. You can close with an affirmation of your own, or you can use this one:

We have learned and believe that agreeing wholeheartedly with each other, loving one another, and working together with one mind and purpose are the ways to achieve unity. We will pursue unity in our marriage and in our family. As conflicts arise, we will remember to seek wisdom and truth in everything. When we are divided, we will use wisdom to recognize the source of our division, humility to swallow our pride, and patience in responding to each other. We will seek truth and remove destructive thought patterns that magnify situations and create discord. We will be intentional in our blending and will pursue unity. Our family will become one.

Commit to saying this affirmation together at least twice more this week.

3

BETTER THAN MENDED

You will live by your sword and you will serve your brother. But when you decide to break free, you will shake his yoke from your neck.

Isaac, a Hebrew Father

All of us have places of pain in our lives that hinder our moving forward as healthy individuals and members of our families. This week we want to begin to open up those places, seek truth intensely about them, and begin healing so that we can thrive within our families as we become whole.

DISCOVERY

IDENTIFYING AND BEING FREED
FROM OUR PAIN

If you and your spouse have been married for any length of time—from one day to fifty years—you know that being a blended family has its fair share of challenges, some great and some small. Sometimes these challenges become heavy weights that we carry throughout the course of our marriages.

We don't always mean to drag these frustrations and issues with us, and every once in a while we even seem to forget that they are there. Yet at any given moment, something can trigger a painful memory, and hurt can rise up within us. Suddenly we realize that we have been carrying this pain with us as a heavy weight attached to our hearts.

Before we can move forward in our journeys to have families that are better than blended, we must identify any weight we are carrying that is affecting our relationship with our spouses, children, stepchildren, or other family members and may be hindering us from fully embracing our blended families.

This chapter is one of the most important of this book. Its goal is to offer tools that will help us experience wholeness and healing so that we can fully embrace our blended families. In order for healing to happen, we must address our areas of brokenness.

To shed some light on these areas in our lives and get some great tools to help us in the healing process, we will use a story from the Bible. While this book is not necessarily religious in nature, this story illustrates the teaching for this chapter in a very clear way.

A STOLEN FUTURE

In the book of Genesis there is a story about two brothers named Jacob and Esau. When their father, Isaac, knew he was close to death, he called for his oldest son, Esau, to come see him. It was the custom then, as it is now in some cultures, for the oldest son to receive the family blessing. Now to us the blessing may not sound like much, but in Jacob and Esau's culture, it had great value. It represented the passing down of wealth, responsibility, and leadership. It was similar to a king passing on his kingdom to his son when he died. It was huge!

When Esau went to prepare for that special moment (which included making a specific meal that his father had requested and a few other things), Jacob, coerced by his mother, decided to trick his father into giving him the blessing. Isaac was old and blind and relied strongly on touch, hearing, and smell to help him recognize what was going on around him, and Jacob used this to his advantage, presenting his father with exactly what was needed to convince him that he, Jacob, was in fact Esau. He made himself smell and feel like Esau, and although the sound of his voice was a little off, old age could play tricks on someone's mind, right? After a certain level of persuasion, Isaac ended up believing that Jacob was Esau and gave Jacob his older brother's blessing.

What a terrible moment it was for Esau when he found out! He felt angry, hurt, betrayed, and lost. He begged his father to take the blessing back from Jacob, but the blessing could not be taken away once it had been given. There was no way to undo it, and there was nothing left for Esau to receive from his father.

Isaac tried to comfort Esau, even though he was quite hurt that Jacob had deceived him. As he spoke to his oldest son, he said several words that are essential to our own next steps in experiencing healing from the pain of the past and present. Isaac said to Esau, "You will live by your sword, and you will serve your brother. But when you decide to break free, you will shake his yoke from your neck."

WHAT ARE OUR SWORDS?

For Esau, his sword was the hurt from his brother, Jacob, stealing the blessing that had been rightfully his as the oldest brother. His father was telling him that he would choose to carry the sword with him.

We all carry a "sword" of some kind. Often this is something from our past, or it could be something that has happened within our blended family. The problem is, we live by the very thing that holds us captive. The swords that we hold onto within our marriages affect our actions and interactions with our spouses. They determine how we love, engage, and accept things within our lives. Unknowingly or knowingly, we filter things through the lenses of our pain. Although our swords may represent something from the past, they can become a strong part of the present and, if left unattended, will creep into the future.

Our swords shape our view of life, of family, and, more than we know, of how we interpret truth. What hurtful mind-sets are you holding onto from your childhood, past relationships, or present relationships that are hindering you and your family?

WHAT ARE OUR YOKES?

Esau's father not only told his son that he would live by his sword, but he also told him, "When you decide to break free, you will shake [your brother's] yoke from your neck." A yoke binds or connects one thing to another. While a sword is something we hold, a yoke is something that holds us. You see, as long as we hold onto our swords, we allow ourselves to be bound by a yoke.

Esau's sword was the hurt his brother had caused him, but the yoke that resulted from his hurt was unforgiveness. The yoke of unforgiveness would send Esau far away from the favor he could have experienced until he decided to let go of his sword—his hurt—and thus be freed from his yoke.

Letting go of our swords isn't always easy, but dragging a yoke along with us isn't either. Yokes can surface as physical illnesses, mental illnesses, seclusion, isolation, fighting, and much more. They have a major impact on our families and on how we embrace our children. The yokes we haul can be passed on from generation to generation.

In order to be productive members of our families, we must decide that we want our blended families to be yoke breakers, not yoke bearers. We must have a desire to break free from our yokes and release our swords.

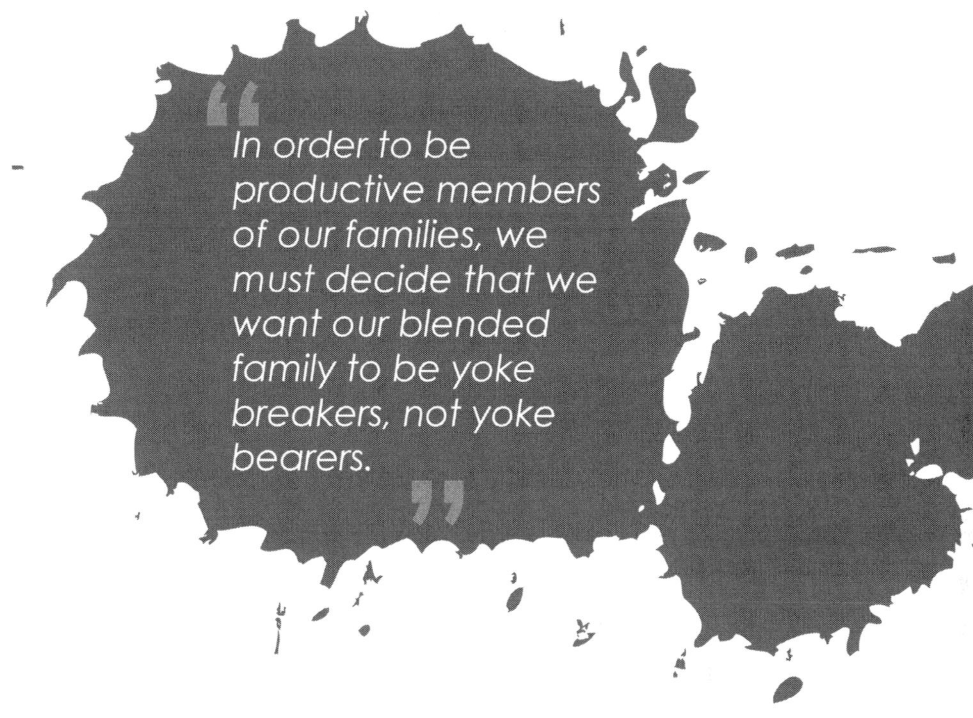

THERE IS HEALING!

What if Esau hadn't been denied his blessing? Or what if the words his father spoke over his life were the greater blessing? "When you decide to break free, you will break his yoke from your neck."

What does breaking free look like? In Esau's case it looked like forgiveness. In essence, the father was telling Esau, "When you decide to stop carrying unforgiveness toward your brother, you will have even greater favor and protection." This is true in our blended families.

In order for us to experience the true beauty of being a blended family, we must decide to release the things we have been carrying from within our families and from the past. We must decide to break free of all the swords and yokes that try to keep us from moving forward.

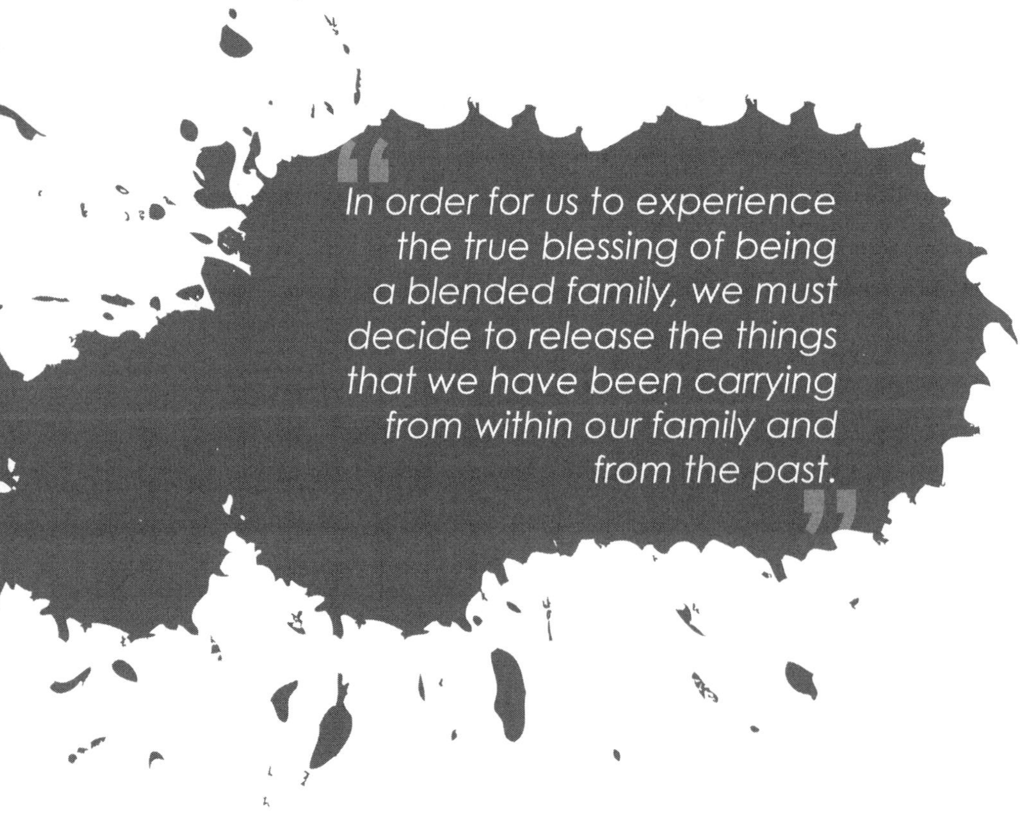

This is something that no one can do for us—but when we do it, everyone will benefit from our decision, even the person or people who hurt us.

DISCUSSION:

HOW DOES THIS APPLY TO OUR SITUATION?

It's time to talk about what we've learned! Pair up with one or two other couples to answer and then discuss the questions below. (If you are uncomfortable talking with others or if you are doing this study at home, you can do this section with just your spouse.) Take ten to fifteen minutes to write your answers individually to the questions below, and then take an additional twenty to thirty minutes to discuss your answers with your spouse and the others in your group.

1. What swords are you holding onto, and what yokes are holding you because of them? In other words, if you let go of your swords, what yokes will you be freed from?

2. What experiences from your past may cause you extreme guilt or pain every time you think of them? How are these swords and their resulting yokes affecting your family's blending process?

3. What areas within your blended family are in need of healing?

4. Who might you need to forgive or to ask forgiveness from?

5. How will forgiving others cause you to break free from your burdens? What will breaking free look and feel like for you?

APPLICATION:

WHAT WILL WE DO DIFFERENTLY NOW?

Session 3 focused on the need for healing and how it affects your blended family. This week, before coming back for session 4, set aside some time at home to complete the action activity below as a couple.

Each spouse should be allowed to explain his or her thoughts regarding the following questions and/or activities. Speak honestly. Listen to each other respectfully.

1. Healing can be instant for some, but for most it is a process. What are some actions you will take to make sure you are healing individually and as a family? Record your plan below.

2. Revisit the family goal you made in session 1, and decide how healing as a family will make a difference in your journey. Create a journal, and record your family goal and your plans to pursue healing so that you can work toward attaining it. Share your findings with your accountability couple, and plan to check in with them frequently.

As you wrap up your application time together as a couple, spend some time together discussing the developing goal you have for your family. You can close with an affirmation of your own, or you can use this one:

We understand that healing is a marathon and not a sprint. We will walk the path of healing with patience and persistence. We will walk the path of forgiveness, learning to embrace every wound and scar as an opportunity to grow in wisdom and character. We will not be content with masking or covering our pain but instead will seek complete and total healing. Whether we have carried our hurts for days, years, or decades, we will seek freedom, peace, and love and will no longer allow our past hurts to dictate our future success. We will be healed and whole as truth becomes the driving force in our pursuit to draw closer to each other. Our family will be one.

Commit to saying this affirmation together at least three more times this week.

4

FIGURING OUT OUR ROLES

*Be a light, not a judge. Be a model,
not a critic.*
Stephen R. Covey

Being part of a blended family is exciting, rewarding, and confusing all at the same time. One of the greatest challenges we face within a blended family is understanding the roles we play in the lives of each individual family member. The role we may have assumed we were to fulfill can quickly change to something else as we begin to better understand the personalities and needs of our spouses and children.

DISCOVERY

UNDERSTANDING THE ROLES OF SPOUSE, PARENT, AND STEPPARENT

While every parent wears a lot of hats, becoming a blended family requires us to fill a few more roles than those required of traditional parents. Sometimes we feel pulled in various directions, and some roles can vie for dominance over others. When we identify our different roles within the family and order them correctly, it will help our marriages and families flourish.

FOCUSING ON OUR SPOUSES

Something often forgotten in a blended family is that the most important role in the home we are to fulfill is the role of a spouse.

It's vital that we understand this, because only when we clearly understand that our role as a spouse is our primary and most important role in the home will we have the greatest impact within our family. The greatest difficulties arise when spouses don't understand this important reality.

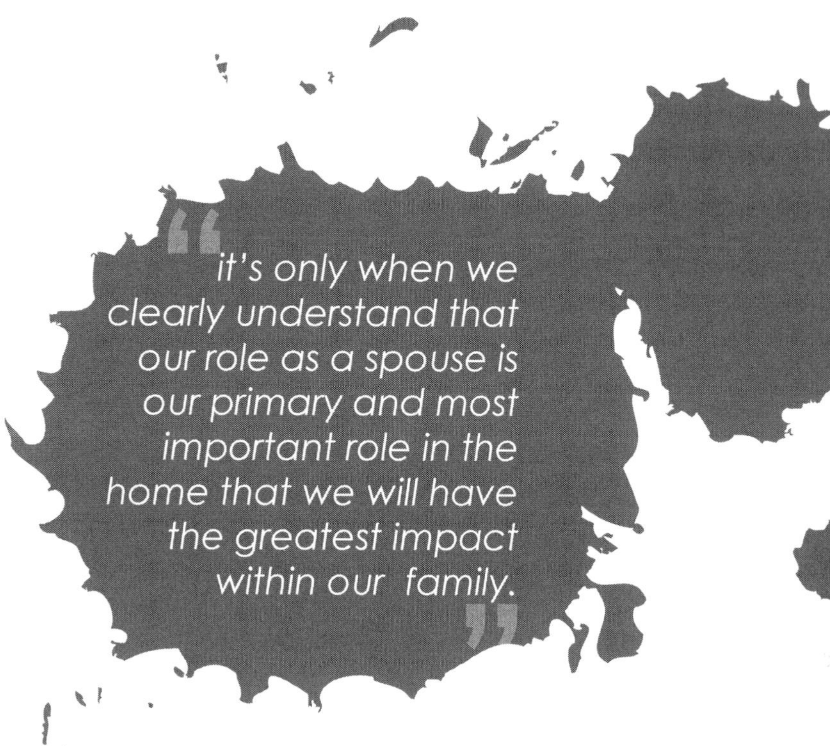

No matter how long we were a single parent, our children must learn that they are no longer first. But most important, we must learn that our children are no longer first. At the point of marriage, we became one with our spouses, and that oneness should not be infiltrated.

Oneness means being accountable to one another, talking through things together, and always seeking what is best for the family before responding to a need. Making our role as spouse our primary one is something that we must constantly be working on as the demands of children and life pressure us to make our marriages secondary.

We will talk more in session 6 about ways that we can keep our marriage relationships in the forefront of our family life.

OUR RELATIONSHIP WITH OUR STEPCHILDREN

It can be a heavy weight when we try to be to our stepchildren what they don't need us to be in their lives. Sometimes we feel pressure from our spouse or from others to be what they believe is missing in a child's life. But we can quickly become overwhelmed, frustrated, and resentful because of the rejection that comes with filling a role that was never ours to fill. Let's take a step back, clear our minds of all the things we thought we had to be in the lives of our stepchildren, such as stepmom or stepdad, and see what we should actually be.

Having a proper order in the home will determine the ultimate success of those who are members of the family. A home is much like a company. There is a CEO (the husband), who governs all the affairs and is held to the greatest level of responsibility within the company. There is a manager (the wife), who maintains and oversees the daily operations of the company. And there are supervisors (the children), individuals who fulfill specific roles within the business, ensure that the mission of the business is fulfilled, and train to become owners of their own company one day. If we take as much time to learn the business of our families as companies take to learn how to have successful businesses, we will see our families grow and thrive just like flourishing companies.

As we learn the business of our homes, we will grow in understanding that our roles are not defined by our positions but rather by our purpose in the home. It is easy for us to get so wrapped up in the title of stepparent that we forget that our number-one and most important role in the lives of our stepchildren—and our biological children as well—is simply to be an example of truth and love in the home.

In other words, we are to show our children that we are striving to make truth the compass that guides all the interactions in our home and in our hearts. This means that love, forgiveness, and grace should be constantly shown through us. People respond to and remember things that they see more than what they hear.

> *It is easy for us to get so wrapped up in the title of stepparents that we forget that our number-one and most important role in the lives of our stepchildren—and our biological children as well—is simply to be an example of truth and love in the home*

Now this doesn't mean that we have to be perfect. It is important that our children see our flaws and shortcomings as well as our good qualities so that they can better understand what it looks like to walk in love, truth, and forgiveness. As we grow in wisdom, our kids should see our growth and should experience the byproduct of unity that is a direct result of this growth. They should be drawn to our pursuit of love because of how we live it out loud in front of them, regardless of any rejection we may have experienced from them.

Our primary role in the lives of our stepchildren and children is to be an example of truth, hope, love, and wisdom.

What does it mean to be this kind of example in our blended families? It simply means that we should focus on showing our stepchildren how to respond to moments of pain, hurt, and rejection with unconditional love. Although they have other parents or relatives in the picture, we have to realize that we are the only ones who can show them how a wife should love their father unconditionally or how a husband should love their mother unconditionally. When we and our spouses begin to have children together, we will be the only ones who can show our older stepchildren and children how to raise their little brothers and sisters in a way that allows them to experience the uniqueness and power of redemptive love. No one else can stand in these places—they were specifically assigned to us—and we have the privilege of modeling this to our stepchildren and children through these relationships. This consistent expression of love will be a natural relationship generator. We (Willie and Rachel) have seen this happen in our own family, and we truly believe that when family members clothe themselves in love for each other, it binds them all together in perfect harmony.

So now we have permission to take off the heavy weight of being Mom or Dad to children who may not need those roles fulfilled, and instead we can just be people who will love our stepchildren, learn about them, and focus on expressing unconditional love toward them and those important to them. As they watch this exchange of love, one day they will desire to experience the same expression of love from us and will be willing to give it back to us.

So what does love toward our stepchildren look like? It is showing acceptance despite any rejection they may have shown toward us. It is showing love even when our stepchildren may not show it in return. It is choosing to express our love for them. It is not forcing ourselves into their world but being patient and understanding. It is accepting the truth that any rejection we feel from our stepchildren is an external expression of their internal pain, and it is being willing not to return rejection for rejection. Showing love toward our stepchildren is accepting them when we have felt rejected by them. Love understands that there is purpose in our position in our stepchildren's lives, and as we seek wisdom and truth, that purpose will be more clearly defined. Love is being willing to grow, learn, experience life with, and enjoy our stepchildren, because love does not dominate—love leads!

The way we develop a relationship with our stepchildren is in being willing to love them even when they seem unlovable or don't desire our love. It is in such moments that our love opens the doors of their hearts, and we grow with them, learn from them, experience life with them, and enjoy them. We aren't forceful or pushy, but we are always available, understanding that love leads.

OUR RELATIONSHIP WITH OUR BIOLOGICAL CHILDREN

When we take our biological children from a state of "just us" to "all of us," we as parents ponder what our relationship with our biological children should look like. Becoming a blended family is a perfect opportunity to instruct our children regarding the importance of change. Children need to understand that change in life is inevitable and necessary. Yet a change in circumstances doesn't mean a change in heart.

The best thing we can do to continue to nurture the relationship with our children is to try not to overcompensate because they are experiencing change. Although we may feel that giving them whatever they want is the solution to how they are responding to the change, that sends them the message that when change happens, they will be rewarded for not learning to adapt to it.

This is not the message we want to send our kids. Instead, we should walk with them through the change and reassure them that our love for them keeps growing every day.

Receiving reassurance in a time of change always makes the change a little more bearable. Children need to know that as they embrace the change taking place in their family, certain good things will remain the same. Even as adults we need that. Just think about a presidential debate. The candidates may have plans to change a lot of things, but the people need to know which good things they plan to maintain from the current government. So our relationship with our biological children should be one of continuously growing love, understanding, patience, and encouragement to embrace the new.

DISCUSSION:

HOW DOES THIS APPLY TO OUR SITUATION?

It's time to talk about what we've learned! Pair up with one or two other couples to answer and then discuss the questions below. (If you are uncomfortable talking with others or if you are doing this study at home, you can do this section with just your spouse.) Take ten to fifteen minutes to write your answers individually to the questions below, and then take an additional twenty to thirty minutes to discuss your answers with your spouse and the others in your group.

1. What expectations have been placed on you in regard to being a stepparent? How have those expectations made you feel?

2. How would you define your role as a stepparent? How do you think your stepchildren feel about being part of a blended family?

3. How do you think your biological children feel about you being part of a stepfamily?

4. What can you do to help foster your relationship with your biological children as well as with your stepchildren?

5. How can you reassure your biological children of what will remain the same about your relationship with them?

APPLICATION:

WHAT WILL WE DO DIFFERENTLY NOW?

Session 4 focused on finding your role in a blended family. This week, before coming back for session 5, set aside some time at home to complete the action activity below as a couple.

Each spouse should be allowed to explain his or her thoughts regarding the following questions and/ or activities. Speak honestly. Listen to each other respectfully.

1. Discuss with your spouse plans for a family activity that will help bring some of your children's needs and questions out into the open and draw your family together:

- *Schedule time for a family day.*

- *Find an activity or a game, such as Monopoly, that takes time and will allow for family discussion during the game.*

- *Have a meal prepared after the activity or game, and plan for everyone to sit together to talk. Encourage everyone to be open with each other about what challenges they may be facing with blending and what they feel would help them during this process.*

- *Be sure to acknowledge each one's feelings, but speak life to each person as well.*

2. Do an activity together to prepare for next week's session. Go online and visit Active Parent Publishing at http://www.activeparenting.com/Parents-Parenting_Style_Quiz, and take the quiz you find there (if you can't find the quiz, search for another quiz that will help you identify your unique parenting style). What is your parenting style—aggressive, passive, autocratic, or permissive? What is your spouse's parenting style? Write this down for each of you, and discuss it together before attending session 5 next week.

3. Revisit the family goal you made in session 1, and create a family-values statement answering the question "What characteristics define our family?" Decide where to display this document in your home. Update your journal with additional needs and/or concerns regarding your family goal. Share these with your accountability couple.

As you wrap up your application time together as a couple, spend some time in discussion together about the developing goal you have for your family. You can close with an affirmation of your own, or you can use this one:

We are thankful for the opportunity to have a fresh start with our blended family. We will grow in love and mutual respect for one another. We will take time to learn about each other as we learn from one another. We will respond to rejection with acceptance. We will learn how to handle conflict and celebrate success together as a family. In the times when we are not certain of our direction we will draw close to the truth, seek wisdom, and draw nearer to each other. Our family will become one.

Commit to saying this together at least four more times this week.

5

DISCIPLINE MEANS DISCIPLESHIP

Discipleship is bringing someone's life
back into order.

Rowel A. Violenta

Frustrations can arise when we blend a family and don't consider some of the practical things that should be adjusted because of the new family dynamic—things like schedules, activities, and boundaries. When we set out to become better than blended, it is vital that we reassess our family priorities and make adjustments where necessary to help our homes run more smoothly. In other words, we need to set some rules.

Some of this is just practical common sense—after all, we need to keep track of who is going where and doing what. But setting guidelines in the home is about more than keeping order. It's about training our children to be disciplined, obedient, and wise. It's about discipleship.

DISCOVERY
DISCIPLING CHILDREN INTO ADULTHOOD

As we work intentionally toward unity in our blended family, we need to consider a major factor: not all children are alike. In fact, they are all uniquely different, and with their different personalities come differences in personal needs. When it comes to blended families, one size does not fit all.

ONE SIZE DOESN'T FIT ALL

Let's take a look at some things blended families may need to consider adjusting:

- *School.* Some children do best in public schools, while others thrive at home school or in a private school. Consider what will be best for each individual child in this important area of their lives. Be flexible!

- *Worship and Religion.* Taking into consideration how your religious practices will impact your family and the best place for your family to worship is vitally important. The place where you chose to express your worship before you married may not work with your new family dynamics. You will want to find a place where everyone can be built up and grow in the truth. Seek wisdom, and talk together about the right place for your family to worship.

- *Bedtimes.* Agreeing upon a time when you and your spouse would like everyone to be in bed is important. The best way to set this up when you have children of different ages is to do a staggered bedtime. This will allow the older kids to feel as if they have received special privileges and will give the younger kids something to look forward to in the future. Stagger the bedtimes starting from the time you would like everyone to be in bed. If that time is eight o'clock, then the youngest should start to go to bed at seven, while the oldest children should have until eight.

- *Outside activities.* Some children enjoy sports, while others enjoy just hanging out with friends. Understanding that each child is unique will help you not to feel that you have to do something for one child just because you did it for another. Some activities cost more than others and require more time. If your goal is to support each child, then understand that this support will look different for each one. For one it may require more of a monetary element, while for another it may require showing up to his or her performance.

WHAT ARE OUR PARENTING STYLES?

While it is helpful for us to adjust family schedules and activities, things will not go smoothly all the time. In the course of family life, we will inevitably have to deal with behavioral issues in our children, and it's important for us to consider the best way to do that.

The beautiful thing when a couple decides to get married is that two people from two different walks of life come together to live life together. The challenge, however, is that two different people from two different walks of life come together under one roof to live life together! Do you see the problem as it relates to parenting? Two people who have been parented by different people will have different parenting styles. Our parenting style is a mixture of how we were raised (our parents' style), what we like and dislike about how we were parented, and what we have learned along the way from our own life experiences.

One of the most important things we can do is understand our own parenting style. Are we a passive parent or a strong disciplinarian? There are many resources that can help us learn our parenting style. One useful free tool, as we saw in the previous session's "Application" section, is a quiz created by Active Parenting Publishers.

(If you did not do this quiz in advance of today's session, stop to do it now, if your class structure allows for it. If it does not, carry on with the session, and do the quiz later at http://www. activeparenting.com/ Parents-Parenting_Style_Quiz.)

Once we figure out whether we have a passive or authoritarian parenting style, it's important for us to discover whether or not our style works within our home and, if it doesn't, to find out what other styles should be considered. It is so easy for us to fall into the trap of parenting in the same way we were raised or, on the other hand, attempting to parent in the complete opposite direction, only to find out that in the end our methods were not best for our children.

As parents, we need to take time to gauge what is working in our home, because the goal of parenting is to raise our children to become adults with integrity and honor and to prepare them for life outside the home so that they can become well-rounded citizens within society. We can know whether or not our parenting style is working if the way we are parenting provides our kids with what they need to fulfill these goals.

DISCIPLINE—PUNISHMENT OR DISCIPLESHIP?

It is important as parents for us to handle our children's behavioral issues in ways that leave both spouses comfortable. In order to do this, we need to talk about our personal expectations as to how we should respond to our children's behavior. In a home that is being guided by the goal of becoming better than blended, the word "discipline" actually means "discipleship." These two words look and sound similar—and that is because they are. The problem is, we often misunderstand the true meaning of the word "discipline." Take a look at the differing views below:

- *Discipline as punishment.* This view is more focused on a child's behavior as the issue and on providing a reaction to an action, which often means punishing simply for the sake of punishing. The focus of this example is solely to dole out consequences, regardless of their actual impact on the child's behavior.

- *Discipline as discipleship.* This view pursues the root of a child's behavior and not just the behavior itself. Discipleship considers why the behavior took place, what lesson needs to be learned, and what needs to be done to see the behavior changed. The focus of this approach is correction that may result in a consequence that is unpleasing to the child but will change the child's behavior.

The primary focus of discipleship is to teach someone the right (or expected) way to live so that they will correct any unhealthy or unproductive behavior patterns. This is what discipleship should look like in the lives of our children. When we allow discipleship to guide us in handling behavioral issues within the home, we avoid reacting in the moment and instead seek wisdom on how to respond to the situation.

Then as a couple we can decide to be open to trying new things as we allow discipleship to take the lead!

This is what King Solomon (a king in Israel from 970 to 931 BC) was driving home when he said, "Direct your children onto the right path, and when they are older, they will not leave it" (the book of Proverbs). This simple truth about discipleship will help us set our children on the right path toward becoming loving and wise children within our homes.

DISCUSSION:

HOW DOES THIS APPLY TO OUR SITUATION?

It's time to talk about what we've learned! Pair up with one or two other couples to answer and then discuss the questions below. (If you are uncomfortable talking with others or if you are doing this study at home, you can do this section with just your spouse.) Take ten to fifteen minutes to write your answers individually to the questions below, and then take an additional twenty to thirty minutes to discuss your answers with your spouse and the others in your group.

1. What are some areas of your blended-family life in which you need to realize that one size doesn't fit all?

*2. What was your parents' style of parenting—
passive or authoritarian?*

*3. What is your parenting style, and from what
sources do you think this was adapted?*

4. How do you and your spouse currently handle behavioral issues within your home?

5. How can your methods of discipline be changed to better foster the goals of raising loving and wise children to become loving and wise adults and to prepare them for life outside the home so that they can become well-rounded citizens within society?

APPLICATION:

WHAT WILL WE DO DIFFERENTLY NOW?

Session 5 focused on discipline versus discipleship. This week, before coming back for session 6, set aside some time at home to complete the action activity below as a couple.

Each spouse should be allowed to explain his or her thoughts regarding the following questions and/ or activities. Speak honestly. Listen to each other respectfully.

1. Discuss as a couple how your parenting styles have impacted your relationship with each other positively or negatively.

2. Talk about the kinds of responses to behavioral issues you are comfortable with versus the kinds you're not comfortable with. Explain to your spouse the reason you feel this way.

3. Come up with two or three ways in which you can respond to issues with the goal of discipline as discipleship rather than discipline as punishment.

Write your answers below.

4. Revisit the family goal you made in session 1, and think about how things have changed in your marriage and family during the past five weeks. Record your reflections in your journal. What changes would you like to see happen in the next five weeks? Share your goals with your accountability couple.

As you wrap up your application time together as a couple, spend some time together talking about the developing goal you have for your family. You can close with an affirmation of your own, or you can use this one:

We have all been created uniquely. We have all been created differently. We believe that we are fearfully and wonderfully made. We will treasure our differences as we seek to honor each of our family members. We will be disciplined in our lives and let our lives serve as a tool to disciple others. We will draw closer to truth and each other. Our family will become one.

Commit to saying this together at least five more times this week.

6

MAKING TIME FOR FAMILY TOGETHERNESS

Yesterday ended last night. Today is a brand-new day and it's yours!

Zig Ziglar

We have spent five weeks discussing ways to become better than blended, and for our final week, we are going to talk about ways to stay better than blended. The key to a peaceful, joyous blended family is to love each other intentionally and, in so doing, create a story that can be shared together for years to come. We do this by deliberately making time to be together in enjoyable and meaningful ways.

As families invest in experiencing life together, they will grow together, love each other more deeply, and bond with each other. All these are essential elements to being a family that will want to be around each other later. We don't want our families to just exist and tolerate each other but to live with and love one another now as well as when they grow older!

DISCOVERY

CREATING WAYS TO BOND AS A FAMILY

Family time can take many forms—sometimes fun, other times more serious. Both are important. Let's look at several ways we can make time for family togetherness and deepen our family relationships.

FINDING TIME FOR FUN!

What better way to bond and become closer as a family than to have fun together! This could mean anything from playing outside in the yard or at a park to playing board games around the kitchen table. The goal isn't about what we do but about growing closer because we are doing it together.

As we make time for our family to have fun together, we create memories that will last a lifetime. Making memories can happen by accident, but they should happen on purpose. When we spend time together with our families, we need to make each moment count. Being intentional now will produce a later harvest of well-nurtured relationships and friendships within the family.

Making memories can include things like going on family vacations or creating holiday traditions. It could mean baking cookies, doing a craft project, or just being willing to play hide-and-seek or Legos with our kids. All these things give our family members something to talk about later and memories to carry with them as they grow up.

KEEPING THE ROMANTIC FLAME BURNING

As we mentioned in session 4, our marriage is our priority relationship in our families. Many times we become so focused on blending with our children and learning about them that we forget to invest in learning about and spending time with our spouse.

But no matter how busy life gets and how many demands are placed upon us, we need to always remember that our first priority relationship is with our spouse.

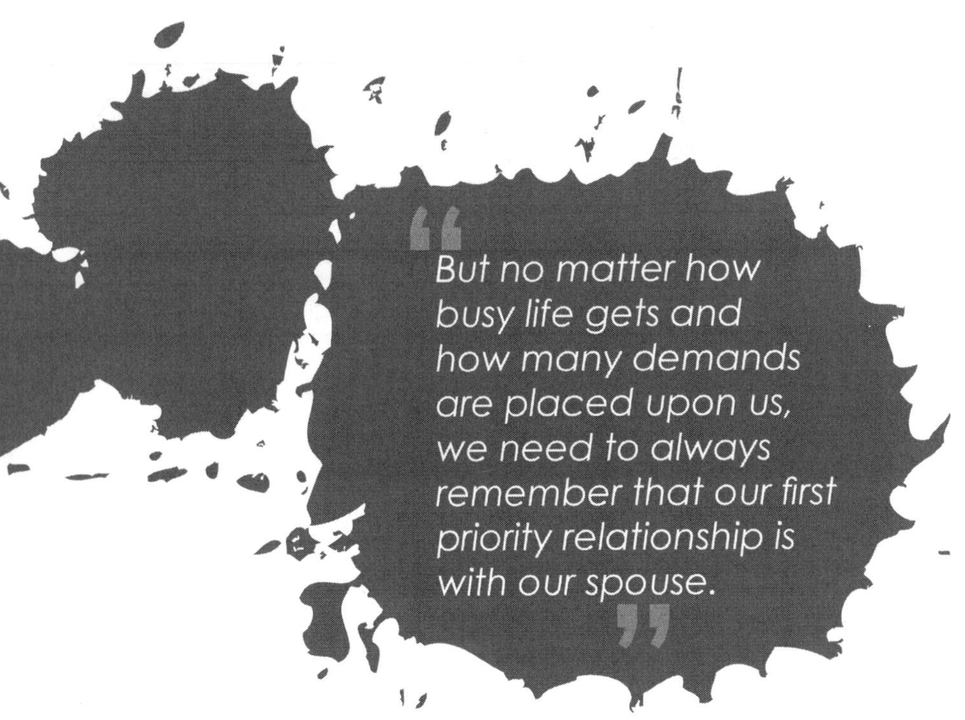

To make our spouses our number-one priority in the family, sometimes we have to remind ourselves that we are parents to X number of kids but the husband or wife of just one person. This means that we have to be intentional with our marriage relationship, because it can easily fall to the bottom of the list. It is our job to preserve our marriages and to be proactive in making time for our spouse.

How do we preserve our marriages as our priority relationship? Here are some tips:

1. Put the truth first. It should be the most important thing that exists in our marriages.

2. Set time aside each evening for you and your spouse to talk to each other about your days.

3. Be open to what your spouse needs.

4. Listen attentively to what's going on in your spouse's life.

5. Hire a reliable babysitter for date nights.

6. Plan date nights—and stick to them.

7. Plan a night away (or a few nights) to rekindle the flames.

8. Learn about something that interests your spouse so that you can engage in his or her interest.

9. Flirt with each other as much as possible.

10. Make communication a priority.

DEFINE WHAT YOU STAND FOR!

We have made it to the end of this first stage of becoming better than blended! The path you have taken to this point came with much dedication, wisdom, and perseverance, and it has only just begun. Becoming better than blended is not a one-and-done sprint. It is a marathon, a race that may at times feel impossible to endure, but it will be easier now that you have some tools to help you be better.

Being better than blended is about embracing imperfections and learning to become better through them.

Our final step in this process is for you to define what you stand for. What does being better look like for you? Developing a family manifesto will bring clarity to your definition of "better." It will help you during those times when you need to embrace truth over rejection and love over pain. A family manifesto will protect family unity, define family purpose, and teach our children the value of a goal. It is one of the best ways to express what it means to be knitted together by strong ties of love.

A family manifesto is a family's proclamation!

As our families become one and we pursue something better than what we may have been told about how blended families work, what we experienced from our own blended families when we were growing up, or what we may have feared in the past about being a blended family, we must continue to seek wisdom, hope, love, and truth, because it will become the expression of redemptive love that our families need in order to experience oneness and unity.

DISCUSSION:

HOW DOES THIS APPLY TO OUR SITUATION?

It's time to talk about what we've learned! Pair up with one or two other couples to answer and then discuss the questions below. (If you are uncomfortable talking with others or if you are doing this study at home, you can do this section with just your spouse.) Take ten to fifteen minutes to write your answers individually to the questions below, and then take an additional twenty to thirty minutes to discuss your answers with your spouse and the others in your group.

1. What does your family do for fun?

2. Do you and your spouse have a regular date night? How do you make sure that you protect your time together as a couple?

3. What is your family manifesto? How do you plan to teach this to your children so that they know it and live by it?

4. What topic from this study has been most impactful for your family?

5. What changes have you seen in your family over the past six weeks? What changes are you most looking forward to in the future?

APPLICATION:

WHAT WILL WE DO DIFFERENTLY NOW?

Session 6 focused on finding time for fun. As this study comes to an end, it is important to prioritize ways for you and your spouse, as well as for your entire family, to enjoy spending time together. This week, set aside some time at home to complete the application activity below as a couple.

Each spouse should be allowed to explain his or her thoughts regarding the following questions and/ or activities. Speak honestly. Listen to each other respectfully.

1. Plan a family activity, and chronicle the activity with pictures: cook a meal, plan a scavenger hunt, play a game, put on a play, or come up with some other creative idea. Use your creativity to create a unique experience that will help your family grow closer to each other. Enjoy the process!

2. Be intentional about planning regular family time. This could be every night before bed, in the morning before everyone leaves for work or school, or any time that works well for your family.

3. Revisit the family goal you made in session 1, and think about how things have changed in

your family during the past six weeks. What dreams do you have for your family? Record it in your journal. Share your testimony and dreams with your accountability couple.

As you wrap up your application time together as a couple, spend some time together talking about the manifesto you have created for your family. Then you can close with an affirmation of your own, or you can use this one:

We will become the blended family we were created to be. We will remember to seek truth for our identity. In conflict we will seek the gift of peace. When we are wounded, we will seek healing. We will be a family that seeks wholeness individually and collectively. We will welcome discipline so that we can disciple our families and those who witness our blended journey. As we become the family we were created to be, we will enjoy and value fun together as a family. We will be intentional in our blending. We will become one family because we understand what it means to be better than blended.

Commit to saying this together at least six more times this week.

LEADER'S GUIDE

The *Better than Blended Workbook* is a six-week study course for couples who are parenting blended families and who desire to do the best job they can building a unified blended family that doesn't just survive but also thrives! The study is intended to be done in a group setting with a leader (although it can work equally well in a small group of several couples or even with a single couple at home).

This study presents six sessions that cover various topics facing blended families:

1. Discovering their own unique blended-family stories.

2. Dealing with conflict that can develop in a blended family.

3. Healing from past hurts so that they can grow their family in a healthy way.

4. Defining their various roles, such as spouse, parent, or stepparent.

5. Learning the meaning of discipline (it's not about punishment!).

6. Exploring various ways to create family togetherness and closeness.

You, the leader, will have a certain amount of freedom in directing the study as needed for your group. Guidelines are given below, but room is left for you to be sensitive to your group's needs.

Make sure every person has his or her own copy of the *Better than Blended Workbook* and a pen or pencil.

Each session is broken into three sections:

- Discovery
- Discussion
- Application

Discovery (30–45 minutes). This first section is one of your biggest responsibilities as a leader. During this time you will lead the couples attending the study through the teaching presented in each session. The text in the "Discovery" section of the workbook provides the basis for the teaching.

We encourage you to study the material in advance and be prepared to present the teaching along with comments and applications of your own. Or, if you are uncomfortable adding your own commentary to the teaching, you could simply read the text aloud and have the couples read along silently with you. This second option won't fill the time allotted for this section, but you can extend the time by giving couples freedom to interject comments and ask questions as you read.

Discussion (30–45 minutes). Direct the couples to break into groups of two to three couples each for a time of answering questions and discussing the material presented in the "Discovery" section. If a couple is uncomfortable sharing openly with others in the group, they can work as a single couple.

Instruct the couples to spend the first ten to fifteen minutes of the "Discussion" section writing their answers to the questions listed in their workbooks. Following that, they should spend the next twenty to thirty minutes discussing their answers with the other couples in their group.

If the couples are engaging with each other and profitably sharing, the discussion time can be extended beyond the thirty to forty-five minutes as you see fit.

When time is up or when discussion seems to be winding down, call the group back together to finish the session.

Application. This final section is for the couples to do at home together. It includes a question or a challenge of some kind, as well as an activity. It ends with a couples affirmation. Read the "Application" instructions aloud with the group, and be sure everyone understands the assignments. Encourage couples to commit to talking with each other during the week, and encourage them to increase this time each week so that they will grow in the habit of talking through things as a couple for their marriage and their family.

Close the session by leading the group in an affirmation.

A FEW PRACTICAL TIPS

Small groups are perfect settings for building community, having a safe place to open up, and sharing needs. It's also a good venue for reaching out to new friends. So think about how you may want to spend time in fellowship: sharing, encouraging, and helping to build community.

Everyone has a different idea of punctuality these days, but as the leader, it's your job to keep things running smoothly. Starting on time, or after a reasonable time of fellowship, helps get the group focused so that you can make the best use of your time.

As you lead the study, don't be afraid of silence—or of controversy. Every group responds and interacts differently. Take things slowly and give people time to think and listen. Then seek out wisdom and truth before you respond. Don't be afraid to say that you aren't sure about something and that you will look into a resource that may help the person asking the question. This will help you keep things moving or bring things back on topic.

Remember too that a study of this nature is intended to provoke discussion. While the "Discovery" section of the session is largely led by you, the leader, for the "Discussion" section you become a facilitator. Encourage couples to open up, share, and ask questions.

As the couples work through the questions in the "Discussion" section, give them plenty of time to answer the questions and respond to each others' findings. Don't feel rushed. Be open to adjusting the meeting's schedule if you sense that you should address a particular need. Each time you teach the group, the meeting will flow differently, and the challenges the couples face will be different. This is normal.

Encourage the couples to complete the assignments so that they can learn how to communicate outside the meetings. However you want to schedule it into the study, making time for the couples to talk together about things they are learning, about their questions, and about challenges they'll face in applying the material is a huge benefit to the couples and to the group. Even beyond that, we encourage you to have individuals who are equipped to handle marriage issues available to talk with the couples as different issues arise that may not be appropriate to handle in group settings. Also, have resources within or outside the facility to give to the couples as they begin to open up about needs in their lives. (For a good list of resources, see "Resources" at the end of this book.)

Thank you for your willingness to lead couples through the *Better than Blended Workbook*!

APPENDIX 1

How Different Ages Affect Children's Adjustment to Blended Families

Children under 10:

- May adjust more easily because they thrive on cohesive family relationships.
- Are more accepting of a new adult.
- Feel competitive for their parent's attention.
- Have more daily needs to be met.

Adolescents aged 10 to 14:

- May have the most difficult time adjusting to a stepfamily.
- Need more time to bond before accepting a new person as a disciplinarian.
- May not demonstrate their feelings openly but may be as sensitive, or more sensitive, than young children when it comes to needing love, support, discipline, and attention.

Teenagers 15 or older:

- May have less involvement in stepfamily life.

• Prefer to separate from the family as they form their own identities.

• Also may not be open in their expression of affection or sensitivity but still want to feel important, loved, and secure.

Gender differences—general tendencies:

• Both boys and girls in stepfamilies tend to prefer verbal affection, such as praises or compliments, rather than physical closeness, like hugs and kisses.

• Girls tend to be uncomfortable with physical displays of affection from their stepfather.

• Boys seem to accept a stepfather more quickly than girls.

Please note that these are only generalizations. Each blended-family experience may be very similar or very different, but understanding these basic principles will help guide our family expectations.[1]

APPENDIX 2

How Different Stages of Identity Affect Children's Adjustment to Blended Families

Infants and toddlers 0 to 4 years old:

In this stage children are likely to associate most strongly with the parental figures in their lives. Parents, caregivers, and older siblings help to mold their view of life and who they are. Toddlers will mimic behavior to help shape their identity. Having the love, acceptance, and admiration of their parental figures is an important element to their proper growth and to shaping who they are. This stage is very relationship driven.

Children 5 to 12 years old:

At this stage children still tend to mimic their parental figures but are now greatly influenced by friends and other outside influences. They are seeking a greater understanding of who they are and who they desire to become based on the people, places, and things that surround them. They are more likely to express the attitudes and behaviors of people with whom they have relationships or toward whom they gravitate. While young children take the opinions and ideas of others and own them as their own, they remain open to wisdom from their parental figures. They are still developing their understanding of right and wrong. They are learning a lot about relationships through both visual and auditory means.

Teens:

In this stage young people are less connected to their parental figures and instead seek their identity from outside influences. They are more likely to disengage from conversation and develop their own attitude about life as it exists. Much of their interaction with family members will be brief and basic—they often won't open up too much about how they feel or what they are thinking regarding life. Teens' moods are ever changing. In this stage they become visual learners when it comes to understanding relationships. In other words, they are less moved by what they hear people say and more by what they see.

NOTES

Session 2: Dealing with Conflict

1. Rachel Scott, *7 Ways To Deal With Conflict In Co-Parenting*, www.BetterThanBlended.com/product/7-Ways-Deal-Conflict-Co-Parenting

2. Gina Kemp, MA, Jeanne Segal, PhD, and Lawrence Robinson, "Step-Parenting and Blended Families,"HelpGuide.org, September 2015, http://www.helpguide.org/articles/family-divorce/step-parenting-blended-families.htm.

Appendix 1: How Different Ages Affect Children's Adjustment to Blended Families

1. Kemp, Segal, and Robinson, "Step-Parenting and Blended Families."

ADDITIONAL BTB RESOURCES

40&7: A Practical Guide to Having Peace during a Custody Battle

So many people are trudging through the muck of a long and tedious custody battle – barely keeping their head above water. The emotions can drain every ounce of mental and emotional energy and deplete us of any reserve we thought we had. What was once an easy task, like sleeping and waking, become more challenging than ever as each new day brings a new concern. The thoughts, the actions, the lawyers, and the daily grind grow into a tornado of chaos removing you far away from the peace that you once knew.

Anxiety, Stress, Frustration and Fear. Sound familiar?

If you grabbed this book, it's probably because you or someone you know may be struggling through a custody battle. Are you searching for something no lawyer, judge or advocate has been able to give? Are you in need of some peace?

Good news! You can have peace during your custody battle! There is a way to experience such peace that you are fully present for your family, fully functioning at work and completely trusting in God during the process!

The tools you will need to experience that peace can be found in this 40&7 book and Scripture Companion journal.

This book will guide you in experiencing the peace your heart is longing for and that God desires you to have. So won't you join me on this journey? Together we will learn how to walk the path of peace during this raging storm.

When conflict comes to us, it's easy to feel a need to respond by saying exactly how we feel. This is a natural human response, especially when we feel attacked in our parenting (be the accusation true or untrue). It wasn't until my friend encouraged me to respond to all the nasty text messages with a simple "OK" or by saying nothing at all that I was able to defuse conflict with my children's birth father. Saying nothing was like blowing up a balloon and then letting go of the end to watch the air seep slowly out of it. Conflict had no place to go but away.

The high-conflict parent thrives off our responses, and when we don't give him or her any, after a few tries the parent stops fighting in the ring alone. *7 Ways to Deal with Conflict in Co-Parenting* gives you practical ways and real-life scenarios to bring control and peace of mind back into your interactions with your children's other birth parent.

Below is a list of websites that have been a help to us in our own blended-family journey. We hope they will be a help to you as well!

Better Than Blended Devotional (YouVersion)

(Available on YouVersion)

Strong blended families aren't the result of some magic pill or a single prayer. Strong blended families require application of the Word of God, willingness to work toward growth, and the ability to apply the wisdom of God in situations! As you read through the Better than Blended 8-Day Devotional, you will find tools that will enhance your blended family experience, strengthen your blended family and marriage, as well as help you to become more intentional with working toward unity and oneness.

40&7: How To Have Peace During A Custody Battle Devotional (YouVersion)

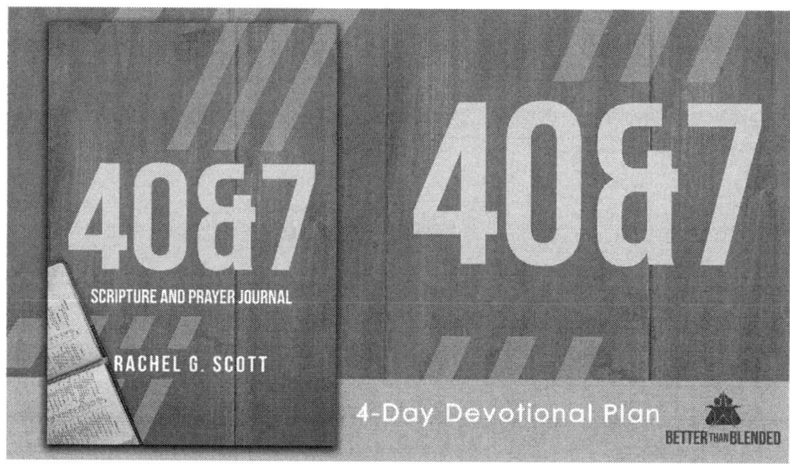

(Available on YouVersion)

Many people are trudging through the muck of a long and tedious custody battle - barely keeping their head above water. The emotions can drain every ounce of mental and emotional energy and deplete us of any reserve we thought we had. The goal of this devotional is to provide you with tools so you can experience peace during your custody battle.

Other Helpful Resources

American Association of Christian Counselors:
www.aacc.net

Families that Win:
www.familiesthatwin.com

Lastleaf:
www.lastleaf.org

HelpGuide.org:
www.helpguide.org

Active Parenting Publishers:
www.activeparenting.com

Stepmom Magazine:
www.stepmommag.com

The Joyful Stepmom:
www.thejoyfulstepmom.com

Dear Homeschool Mom:
www.dearhomeschoolmom.com

Life.Church
www.YouVersion.com
www.Bible.com

Thank you for using the Better than Blended Workbook as a resource guide to becoming a stronger family unit. We hope it has made and will continue to make a difference in the interactions between you and your spouse and with your children. We also hope it has encouraged you to be intentional with each family interaction.

For more information on blended-family resources or to book Willie and Rachel to speak at your venue, visit:

www.BETTERTHANBLENDED.com

or e-mail us at

info@betterthanblended.com

Please follow, share, and comment on our social media sites:

www.facebook.com/betterthanblended
www.twitter.com/BetterThanBlend
www.instagram.com/betterthanblended

Made in the USA
Monee, IL
07 July 2026

56549097R00083